AYDIN'S
PreSchool Years

A Big Brother's Revenge

CAROL L. HINTON

AuthorHouse™
1663 Liberty Drive
Bloomington, IN 47403
www.authorhouse.com
Phone: 1 (800) 839-8640

Published by AuthorHouse 04/27/2019

ISBN: 978-1-5462-4128-7 (sc)
ISBN: 978-1-5462-4129-4 (e)

authorHOUSE®

DEDICATION

This book is dedicated to my Lord and Savior Jesus Christ for His love, kindness, grace, and mercy.

This book is also dedicated to my beautiful, amazing and intelligent, daughter, Tanika, who has an incredible heart and Spirit. Thank you for your invaluable support throughout the process of completing this project, and for giving me two adorable and smart grandsons, Dorian and Aydin. I love and adore you. You mean the world to me.

My sincerest thanks also go to my oldest grandson, Dorian, who allowed me to use him in the book and helped me to write the book. I love and adore you.

I would also like to thank my youngest grandson Aydin, who inspired me to write this book to help him, his big brother Dorian and others, deal with the pain of feeling frustrated, irritated and annoyed with each other. I love and adore you.

ABOUT THE AUTHOR

Carol L. Hinton is a mother, grandmother, author, and most of all a child of God. Carol is the author of Aydin's Preschool Years. For over 20 years, she worked for the Chicago Board of Education. Carol is currently a Licensed Daycare Provider. Carol has donated and given her time, effort, and energy to helping young ones as well as seniors to strive for the best. God has given her many gifts, such as creativity, patience, heart and soul, and energy to work with children. Carol's motto is to treat people like you want to be treated. When she not on the computer working on her next project, she enjoys going to church, playing family games, going on a family outing with her daughter, Tanika, two grandsons Dorian and Aydin, sister Laura, and nephew Jimmy.

CONTENTS

ACKNOWLEDGEMENTS

To My Sweet Daughter
I want to express my special thanks to my beautiful, intelligent daughter for her love, support, encouragement, and help. Tanika is such a positive reinforcement in my life, not to mention, giving me two outstanding, intelligent, funny, talented and very athletic grandsons. Thanks, baby for standing by my side and encouraging me to write the book. I treasure every moment that we are together. I love being your mom.

To My Two Grandsons,
Thanks to my grandchildren, who have inspired me to write the book. For every time I have encouraged you to be more helpful to each other. Thank you, Dorian and Aydin.

To My Late Parents,
I want to extend my sincerest thanks to my beloved and beautiful parents, Mr. & Mrs. Ellis Hinton, for their love, kindness, support, provision, prayers and most of all, for setting a solid spiritual foundation. I love and miss you two.

To My Dearest Sister
Thanks to my amazing twin sister Laura, for believing in me and pushing me to use the gifts God has given me. And also, for her great insight, input, patience, and most of all, helping me to get in touch with my sense of humor side. I am genuinely grateful to her.

To My God-fearing Brother, Pastor Michael Hinton,
who also helped me to keep the faith in the Lord, stand on His Word, and always making me feel like I can do anything, I am truly grateful.

To My Handsome, Funny and Talented Nephew, Jimmy,
who encourages me to keep writing in the wee hours of the night. When I felt exhausted and wanted to give up on writing, you cheered me on.

Thanks to My Wonderful Siblings,
Brenda, Michael, Corine, Laura, and Lolita.

To all of My Nieces and Nephews
for believing in me.

To My Beautiful God Daughter,
Jasmine Gilbert.

Thanks to the Learning Mansion Daycare Parents
for allowing me to use the children in the book.

Thanks to Danielle Porch for encouraging and motivating
me to unleash my creativity. Ms. Danielle Porch, YOU ROCK!!!

CHAPTER 1

The Ugly, Nasty, Ongoing Battle

Getting Revenge on a sibling could devastate a whole family. How do I know? It almost happened to me. My name is Dorian, and my little brother is Aydin, and this is our story. For eight years I was an only kid. I was living the good life. Well, that's how I saw it. I didn't have to worry about anything.

Everything belonged to me. My space, my time, my food, my clothes, my toys at the time, but most of all, my fun-loving parents and every bit of their love and attention. Not to mention there wasn't anyone to irritate me or to compare me to.

It was all about me, me, and me. Until the day I got a new baby brother. At first, Aydin was the best baby brother ever. All he did was eat, sleep and poop just like mom said he would.

But then, he got older and started taking over the whole house. He started demanding things from mom and dad, telling them to do this and do that, sit here and sit there. The bossing around went well into Aydin's preschool years. Aydin's attitude and tone had a shift.

The little boy who could only say "gaga" "goo goo," "pee pee," and "boo boo" was a thing of the past. All he does is talk lots and lots of trash-talk.

I mean, he talks so much garbage that it drives me crazy, to a point where, all we do is battle. Now don't get me wrong, we didn't fist fight, but we battled with our words. Sometimes we have some really ugly, nasty, ongoing battles.

Mom said I should talk nicer and kinder to my little brother rather than raising my voice to him because I'm older and I know better. Well, I probably would mom, if he wouldn't say stupid little things like how I think I got swag but I'm an idiot.

He continued talking about how all my friends are butt heads, how he's the boss of me, how he's going to be stronger, richer, taller, and have a prettier girlfriend, and more money than me, when he gets older. "And you want to know why!" I yelled, "well there you are mom. Aydin goes a bit overboard with the name calling."

My dad said in his baritone parenting voice, "Be a little more patience; things will get better, son." "Well, dad, things aren't getting any better, they're getting worse and my patience for Aydin has run out."

I know it has because when he irritates me now, I would grab that weasel and put him in a headlock, and he would yell and scream to let him go, and of course, mom comes running with a terrified look on her face. And when she saw Aydin in a headlock she said, "Oh my God, you're going to hurt my baby, let him go." "Really mom, we're just playing around," at least that's what I told her.

"Well, find something else to play that doesn't involve putting my baby, in a headlock," mom said. After mom's short, unnecessary lecture, Aydin turned around and said, "Ha-ha!"

He got me in trouble and to top it all off, he called me a big fat loser. And that was my breaking point. I was ready to fight back; this meant war! I just needed to figure out what I was going to do to get revenge on my little brother for all the times he had annoyed me. Actually, what I meant was taking all the attention from me.

So, for two whole weeks, I spent every single day thinking about how to get back at Aydin. However, I couldn't think of anything. I was just about to give up on it, when my friend, Malik, who's in a similar situation suggested giving Aydin the silent treatment, and so, I tried it. Boy, was that a super dumb idea! Giving Aydin the silent treatment that day only made things way worse.

The morning started off incredibly impossible for a silent treatment; Aydin kicked it off by calling me a million, and one times, "Bruh! Bruh! Mom said to wake up big head. Bruh! Bruh! Mom said you're going to be late for school, stupid. Bruh! Bruh! Mom said your breakfast is getting cold, butt head, oh, and Bruh! Bruh! please, please don't forget your deodorant, your underarms be funky!!!"

After Aydin's last silly insult, I had a vision of me, kicking him off my bed, but instead, I remained silent, I got up, wiped the drool from the side of my face, took my shower, brushed my teeth, came back to my room, got dressed for school, and much to my surprise, Aydin was hiding in my closet. He jumped out, grabbed me by my anklets and seriously scared the crap out of me and said, "Aha! I scared you, you are a scary-cat." At the time, I didn't realize all he wanted was for me to spend a little time with him.

But instead of me spending a few minutes with him, I grabbed him by his collar, picked him up, and threw him in my dirty clothes hamper. Of course, he started kicking and screaming, "It stinks in here." By this time, mom had come up the stairs to my room and asked, "What in the world are you doing to him?"

"I'm not doing anything to him, he came into my room bothering me." "I was just trying to tell Bruh Bruh to hurry up because his food was getting cold, like you said." Aydin told mom. "Ok, we gotta go," Mom said. She totally ignored the situation.

Then, later on that afternoon, I was doing my homework, Aydin grabbed mom's hairbrush and pretended it was a mic and started rapping about me, he called the rap, "My Big Brother a Loser," it was hilarious and disrespectful.

I thought he'll wear himself out eventually and give up on irritating me, but not Aydin, that evening I was eating dinner when Aydin started doing cartwheels and flips and knocked my favorite food, off the table, and said to me, "That's what you get for trying to give me the silent treatment today."

I just blew him off and went upstairs to my room and laid across my bed, and drifted off to sleep. I tossed and turned all night. I was dreaming, that I had got so angry with Aydin that I rolled him as flat as a pancake and put him inside a giant envelope and dropped him inside a giant mailbox.

Then a giant mailman collected him and placed him on a giant truck to be delivered to a brand new giant family. I was just so glad to be an only kid again that I didn't realize that the giant family had cooked Aydin and ate him for dinner. I woke up from the bad dream in a state of panic, shaken and wondering whether it was a dream or an actual incident.

Now don't get me wrong. I don't care how many ugly, nasty, ongoing battles we go through, I love my little brother and would do anything for him, however, he has to stop embarrassing me in front of my friends..

Like the time he unleashed a fart in front of my girl and thought it was funny. Sure, it would've been for immediate family only. But, not in front of my girl, I was so embarrassed I couldn't speak. I think Aydin lived to embarrass me.

CHAPTER 2

Here's the Problem

Like this other time, the guys from school were over to the house to work on a science project, but we ended up playing Fortnite on my video game first. I had made it to level seventy-five, feeling really good about it when Aydin walked in my room twirling something around on a stick, chatting.

"Look what I found in the laundry room." At the time, I couldn't tell what it was, then he got closer; it was a pair of my underwear.

Everyone sat spellbound for a moment, and then my friends burst out laughing. They laughed so hard that it made their stomach hurt.

I tried to grab my underwear from Aydin, but I fell flat on my face. Then he tossed the underwear on my head, stuck his tongue out, and said, "Nana nana nana, you can't catch me" and he took off running.

This wouldn't happen if I was the only kid. So I picked myself up from the floor and started chasing after him.

I almost caught him, but he ran into the kitchen where mom was doing some work on the computer, screaming as loud as he could, "Leave me alone, Bruh Bruh!" "Hey! What's all the screaming about?" mom asked Aydin." "Bruh Bruh was chasing me," he told mom.

"Okay, Dorian stop chasing my baby so he won't injure himself," mom said. I didn't say a word; I just walked back to my room. On my way back, I was so angry with my little brother, I said to myself, "Playtime is over."

I was thinking so hard about it; my friends noticed that my head wasn't in the game anymore, and decided they wanted to play basketball. We had been playing for a little while, when Aydin, showed up and insisted on playing.

However, I told him to go and play with a baby toy or something, and of course, he didn't go away. Instead, he yelled out while I was going up for a layup and missed, "You're weak Bruh Bruh, you gotta work on those lay-ups. How could you miss the easiest shot in basketball?"

I started calling Aydin names. And then he jumped on my back. I tried to knock him off, but he grabbed hold of my neck. My friend, Dre suggested to throw him off, but Dre's ideas are a bit bizarre. So I fell to my knees to get Aydin off my back.

But he still wouldn't let go of my neck, so then we rolled around on the floor and ended up knocking mom's favorite floor lamp over.

Mom came running and saw the broken lamp and asked, "What's going on down here?" Aydin looked at me, and I looked at Aydin, and we both looked down at the lamp. Neither one of us said a word. Until dude started laughing, as if something was funny. Which made mom upset.

Then finally, Aydin said, "Bruh Bruh wouldn't let me play ball." Mom tried to maintain a calm face; she said, "Dorian, how many times do I have to tell you all to stop playing rough in the house?" "I asked him nicely to let me play, but he wouldn't listen," said Aydin.

Mom gave me a warning look and walked away. After she cleaned up the broken pieces, she said to me, "I'll deal with you later, come on Aydin." Aydin slowly trailed behind mom so that he could stick out his tongue and say to my friends, "So long losers."

CHAPTER 3

Enough Is Enough

"MAN! Your little brother is too extra," my friend Dre said all at once. I'm glad I don't have one of those, if I did, I would beat him up every day."" Yea, that little dude seems like he loves to get you in trouble," my other friend Xavier added.

"Yea, he does," I said to Xavier. "Well, you know the phrase, you can choose your friends, but you can't choose your brother," said Malik. "It's obvious, you don't know the phrase yourself because you got it wrong, the phrase is you can choose your friends, but you can't choose your family," explained Xavier.

"Well," Malik replied, "I wished I could break that stupid rule because my little brother Ryan is the kid you love to hate."

"Bottom line, I've had more than enough of my little brother's annoying little ways. Enough is enough," I replied. "Yea," said Malik, "we gotta stop them!" "Whatcha goin do about it?" asked Xavier. "I don't know," I said to Xavier. The room got real quiet for a moment of thinking, then Dre shouted.

"BOOM! I got it!" as we eagerly waited for him to answer. "On Monday, our school will be celebrating sibling day."

"Are y'all thinking what I'm thinking?" Dre added. "Yea," I said to Dre, slapping him on the back in a friendly manner. But of course, it took a moment for Malik to understand what Dre was saying. Then he got it. "Oh," Malik says "a perfect opportunity to get even with our little brothers." "Yep!" I said to Malik.

But, are you sure the sibling day is on Monday, Dre?" "I'm not for sure," said Dre, "but I overheard mom talking to another parent from school about it." "Well, ok, I'll spend all day tomorrow working on prank just in case." "Pranks, I love me some good pranks," said Aydin, who sneaked up on us, out of nowhere. "Never mind that! What do you want?" "Mom said it's time to rap things up, it's getting late. So, tell your nerdy friends to call their parents."

"Ok, now get out of my room," I told Aydin in a fed-up voice. "You're not the boss of me," Aydin said. "Yes, I am," I told him. "Now get out!"

After my friends left, I spent the entire evening and the next day preparing for battle.

At first, I felt like I was fighting a losing battle, then Malik called me and suggested to use this hilarious prank, which I thought was a perfect idea.

No one had ever suggested Malik might have a good idea of how to prank someone because he was such a lame.

Finally, Monday morning came. It was the perfect Autumn day! And it was time to give Aydin a taste of his own medicine. I was excited.

But, at the same time, I was getting this gut feeling in my stomach. I almost freak out because I wasn't sure if the school was going to celebrate sibling day especially after I had worked hard and was as prepared as I would ever be for my revenge battle.

As Malik and Dre walked into the classroom, they both took a long hard look at me. So did Xavier.

They were wondering about the pranks I had for my little brother. "Hey, what's the plan?" Dre asked me.

I didn't say anything. I just looked around for my teacher, Mr. Allison, who wasn't in the room yet.

The kids in the classroom were talking and putting their things away. Others were doing things eighth-graders shouldn't be doing, like going inside the teacher's desk, talking on their cell phones, using profanity, and bullying. Just then, the door opened. I had just sat down at my desk and pulled out my school journal.

Then all of a sudden, the principal, a tall, kinda mean, rough, serious looking guy, with big hair, entered the room, followed by Mr. Allison, who said, "Boys and girls!" May I have your attention, please. I got some good news.

"Today is Sibling Day in pre-k, and to help them celebrate, What My Sibling Means to Me. You all are invited to join them in their classroom for this special day."

All of the eighth-graders groaned out loud, all except for Malik and me, it was the best news ever. I was so excited to hear it I jumped up from my seat with the biggest smile on my face and joy in my heart that I began to hug everyone in my classroom even the kids I didn't like, except for the creepy corner kids and the detached kids who ignored the teacher and I began to sing, "Sibling's day in pre-k, Sibling's day in pre-k, sibling day in pre-k..."

And my friend Malik joined in with me because he was happy with the good news as well. Just then, the principal, my teacher and some of our classmates looked straight at us as the words of the song echoed in their ears.

Their strange look on their faces suggested that something was wrong with us. They looked at us as if we were a three-eyed monsters. But they had no idea, why, we were happy.

They didn't understand that we've been waiting for this moment forever. And now that it's here, we couldn't wait to get to our little brothers' classroom.

When we arrived, the preschoolers had just finished their meet and greet routine. They had just set the tone for the whole day.

Immediately, Aydin saw me, his smile dropped, he had a good feeling I was up to something. And he was right. I used my pranks to embarrass him in front of his friends the whole day.

I knew I had gotten my revenge on Aydin when he laid down for a nap and he was literally speechless. It was as sweet as it gets. It felt like I've won the championship game in overtime on a buzzer beater game tied with seconds remaining, and I made this incredible 3-point winning shot.

I was pleased, but, as for my little brother, he was still pretty angry and hurt about the pranking.

CHAPTER 4

Aydin Expressed
His Feelings

When he woke up from his nap, he started throwing chairs, kicking over tables, ripping up books, making growling sounds, slapping erasers together, sending up a white cloud of chalk into the air and causing all the kids to choke.

Okay, I'm stretching the truth a bit, that's not how it happened. Aydin wasn't throwing or kicking over chairs, he wasn't ripping up books, nor did he slap erasers together causing the kids to choke, it just sounds more interesting to say.

Actually, when he got up from his nap, the sweet smell of his favorite banana bread filled the air, but he didn't care; he was grumpy. It was clear that his grumpiness wasn't coming from him being hungry, or not having enough rest, but because he got a taste of his own medicine.

All the kids were eating their banana bread and drinking their milk, but not Aydin. Everyone knows that Aydin loves his snacks. "Hey Aydin, how come you're not eating your snacks," asked Lendon? "Do you feel better?" asked Kareem. Aydin shook his head, no. "Are you still upset about the pranking?" asked Loyal? "Yep!" he said in a frustrating tone.

"Hey, I got a really good idea, maybe if you drink some of your milk it might make you stronger," said a little boy named Georgio. "Nope! I don't want any of it," Aydin said. And he pushed it away, spilling milk everywhere. "Ooh! I'm telling Mrs. Taylor, you spilled your milk," said Belle, the tattle teller.

"Be quiet Belle, it was an accident," Aydin told her. "Know it wasn't," said Belle. "Yes! It was," shouted Aydin. "I'm going to tell her right now," said Belle. "No!" shouted Aydin in a clear, high-pitched voice. He got so irritated with Belle that he put his head down on the table and locked his head into his folded arm!

Because, here's the thing, Aydin is a good kid and doesn't like to get in trouble at school. His teacher always referred to him as an excellent, well-behaved student and never once get into trouble.

For a split second, I wanted to go over and give him a big brotherly hug. Just then, Dre spotted me watching Aydin with his head down, and walked over and whispered, "Dude, I know you're not thinking about going over there to rescue him, are you crazy, did you forget about all of the annoying little things he's does to you?" So, I just smiled and continued to take in the sweet, sweet taste of my victory.

After snack, Mrs. Taylor said, "What an exciting day we had in our classroom today. Before we go, we would like to first, thank our big brothers and big sisters for taking the time to celebrate with us. Would anyone like to introduce us to their sibling and thank them for coming?"

"Meeeee!" shouted Madisyn. She walked toward the front of the class and grabbed her big sister by the hand and said, "This is my sister, Melody, but I call her sissy, I love her a whole lot, and she's my best friend, and I want to thank her for coming."

"Awwww!" said the whole class. Then Maya went next. After Maya came a boy name Ryan Dexter, who loves reading books, then Desmond Daniel, a boy in the class, who licks his snot and eats his boogers. After him, lots of children introduced us to their siblings.

Then Mrs. Taylor asked, "Aydin, would you like to go next." Of course, Aydin quickly shook his head, no! Mrs. Taylor wanted to know why Aydin didn't want to go next. Aydin responded, "Because I got nothing good to say about my big brother."

"He never plays with me, he yells at me all the time. He calls me names, he bosses me around and my big brother spends more time with his friends than he spends with me." Aydin started crying. I thought he was faking, but he really was crying his eyes out. Mrs. Taylor had to provide comfort to Aydin.

I hate too admit it, but I felt very hurt inside. Mrs. Taylor took a really big breath because she couldn't believe what she had heard. Then she told the children it was time to go home.

The kids gathered their book bags, homework folders, and coats, and brought them to the carpet. I was so ready to go because it seemed as though all the little kids were staring at me with a disappointing look on their faces, including Mrs. Taylor.

Instead of them giving each other their end-of-the-day special handshake, they were giving Aydin lots of hugs because he was still crying. It seemed like three o'clock was never going to come.

CHAPTER 5

Aydin's Embarrassing Moment

Then finally, the stupid dismissal bell rang, and I rushed out of the classroom door so fast that I accidentally knocked over a little girl named Madisyn, who hurt her arm. I helped her up and told her I was sorry.

I felt terrible, not just because I accidentally knocked over Madisyn, but because I thought that getting victory over my little brother was everything, but now I know, it wasn't. So, Mrs. Taylor called me back to the classroom to get Aydin's hand. But of course, Aydin didn't want me to hold his hand, and he walked on ahead of me. I pretended like I didn't care, but actually, I felt really hurt inside.

"Aydin! Dorian!" called Mom as she walked toward us, waving with a warm smile on her face, and glad to see her children. As soon as Aydin saw her, a teary eye was forming, but he wouldn't let it out.

Aydin knew if he did Mom would've treated him like a baby in front of the school kids. So Aydin took a deep breath and held back his tears.

I was hoping Mom wouldn't notice that something was wrong with him. But of course, the sadness in his eyes, trigger some ideas. "There's my little Angel face," said Mom, and she lifted Aydin in the breezy air and gave him a big mushy kiss on the cheek. Aydin was stunned. His face became as red as a tomato.

"Mom, please put me down, I've had enough embarrassment in one day," Aydin told her. But, she continued to embarrass him. She started pinching on his cheeks and singing a made-up song of love from her to him in an overly-friendly voice.

Mom can be sweet and even say kind things, but there's a side of her that gets your face turning red with embarrassment.

All Aydin could do was cover his face with his hands. I found it so funny how mom was embarrassing him until she tried to do me. Mom leaned into me for a hug and kiss, in public, so, I had no other choice but to block her.

Then I turned to walk away mumbling to myself, "Man, mom is trippin, I'm in eighth grade and just too cool for this." But deep down inside me, I loved it. But of course, mom never stopped, she continued to embarrass Aydin all the way to the car.

And if things couldn't get any worse for my little brother, out of nowhere came this high screechy voice, "Bye Aydin." Aydin knew that voice anywhere. His mouth flew wide open, and his eyes were as big as saucers.

Because it was Desmond Daniels, the creepy kid from his class who eats his slimy, icky, boogers. Ewww! Gross! I thought to myself.

So Aydin tried to ignore him, but Desmond and his mom started walking fast toward the car. Aydin's heart began to pound fast because Desmond was yelling, "Hey Aydin I forgot to give you our end of the day handshake."

Granny, who was in the front seat of the car quickly unlocked the door and Aydin hopped in the back seat and he ducked all the way down, dodging Desmond and his mom. "Whew! That was a close one!" Aydin whispered.

CHAPTER 6

My Granny's A Spy

Oh my Goodness, love muffin, you look as if you've seen a ghost. What in the world is going on?" asked granny, who eyed Aydin with suspicion.

"Shhhh! Granny, please be quiet, I'm trying to hide from Desmond Daniels." Aydin whispered. "Who in the world is Desmond Daniels? Granny asked. "He's a boy in my classroom everybody call snot-nose Daniel," said Aydin.

"But why are you hiding from him?" Asked Granny, who Bruh Bruh and I suspect is not your typical granny. She's sweet and kind and all, and cooks the best food in the world, next to mom. But we wonder if that lady's a spy.

She's great at getting us to talk about stuff, and she knows a lot about everyone. And she's always watching with those set of eyes. Plus, she carries enormous handbags.

So after, snot-nosed Desmond and his mom pulled out of the parking lot, Aydin let out a big heavy sigh; as in, a sound of relief and frustrations. Granny turned around and asked frantically, "Hey, wait a minute, did that Desmond boy picks on you at school?

"No, Granny, take it easy, you freaking out," Aydin told granny. "Well! What's with the long cute face, it looks a bit upset?" she said? "Seriously, Granny, boys are not cute, they are cool, right Aydin? But, he never answered the question.

I just laughed it off. "Well, anyway," granny said, "I got a BIG surprise that would cheer you up."

"What is it, Granny?" I asked. "Your Papa and I are taking you guys to a basketball game," she said. "Yes! I shouted as I started dabbling in my seat, falling over on Aydin. "Get off me," Aydin said and pushed me away.

"When are we going, Granny?" "In two weeks," she said. "Thank goodness, I thought you were going to say next weekend, that's Aydin's playdate," mom said." "Oh, you were willing to give the whole playdate thing another go.

Even after, that boy, who brought his pet hamster with him and frightened all the kids with it that night. I hope you didn't invite him," said Granny.

"What about that new kid, that lives next door?" I asked mom. Mom rolled her eyes at me and said, "He's not invited either." "Good, he was weirder than weird," I said to mom. "Hey Aydin, remember he snapped the heads off your new wrestlers and flushed them down the toilet.

And mom had to pay a plumber lots of money to fix it." I thought Aydin was going to say, yea, I remember. But, instead, he told me to shut-up and asked mom if we could go home now?

Surely, that wasn't the response I was looking for Aydin to give. "Sure, sweetie," said mom, fasten your seat belt."

CHAPTER 7

On the Ride Home

Aydin reached for his seatbelt, but it wouldn't click. He tried to force it to work. "Are you trying to break mom's seatbelt?" I asked him. "No, I'm not!" he cried.

Mom turned around and told me to help him with his seatbelt, and, I reached around to help and whispered, "Sure, I'll help the little crybaby." Aydin got pretty angry with me, and shouted, "I hate you, Bruh Bruh!"

"Aydin!" shouted Mom, "don't ever let me hear you said that about your brother again?" "But mom," Aydin cried, "Bruh Bruh being picking on me all day."

"Why were you picking on him at school?" asked mom. I had to think of something quick.

I cleared my throat, "Ahem..."as if I was going to respond to the question, but instead, I reached into my backpack and pulled out my test papers.

"Hey, mom, I forgot to tell you and granny, I got an **A+** on my math and science test, see here granny," I said handing her both papers with a large red "A+" on top. Talking about getting good grades, can easily change the subject.

"That's wonderful! Grandson, I'm so proud of you, so very proud," Granny said to me. "Thanks, Granny, show my Momma my papers."

Mom glimpsed quickly at the papers because she was driving. She smiled big and said, "Excellent job, turkey!" A nickname she calls me when she's feeling proud of me.

So, I looked over at my little brother and said to myself, "Don't underestimate the power of being the oldest sibling." Showing Mom my test papers were a smart idea. Because she loves it when I get good grades at school.

I was feeling good at first. Just then, my heart got a little thumpy; worry had kicked in a bit because I'm supposed to go to my friend Xavier's party this weekend, and a high chance, mom could ground me for what I did to Aydin at school.

CHAPTER 8

Feel Like Talking

As soon as Aydin got into the house, he threw his book bag and coat on the floor and stormed up the stairs; his feet sounded as massive as the Hulk. It made the whole house shake.

I didn't say anything. Usually, I would've teased him, or tried to pull him down the stairs, but, I just watched him stomp off to his room.

Although, my little brother and I don't see eye to eye about everything, I felt awful. And I even had some regrets.

Mom and Granny both looked at each other with a worried face because Aydin never goes straight to his room after school, he always raids the refrigerator for some snacks, but not today. Mom sat her purse down and went up stairs to Aydin's room.

"Knock! Knock!" said mom. "Come in," Aydin said to her in a low choked up voice. "Hi, honey, I noticed how upset you were on the ride home. You all right?" she asks. "I don't want to go back to school," Aydin said. "Feel like talking about it?" she asked. Aydin gently rested his head comfortably on Mom's shoulder and said, "I'm upset with Bruh Bruh."

"With Bruh Bruh, for what, sweetheart?" mom asked. "Because, he embarrassed me at school today," he cried. "What do you mean?" asked mom? "Well, he paused, Bruh Bruh followed me around my classroom all morning just to annoy me." "Why was Bruh Bruh in your classroom today?" mom asked. "Remember, it was Sibling Day, in pre-k, mom," said Aydin.

"Oh honey, your brother was just playing around, having a little fun with you," mom explained. "Well, at first, it was kinda fun having him there to play with me.

But, he was only pretending to be interested in showing me how to build a super cool transformer and the best way to connect it, and then it happened, Bruh Bruh planted a whoopee cushion right under my butt, when I wasn't looking, and I sat on it, and it sounded like I let out a big fart."

"EWWWW!" shouted, my classmates, and they walked away laughing at me really hard. "I was so angry with Bruh Bruh that I told him to stay away from me. But of course, he wouldn't leave me alone. He followed me to the dramatic play area where my friends and I were playing house."

"I was pretending to be the daddy and Sofia was the mommy. And sure enough, Bruh Bruh walked over, squeezing himself through the crowd and started singing the nursery rhymes song, Aydin and Sofia sitting in a tree, k-i-s-s-i-n-g, first comes love and then come marriage." "Heeeeey! shouted Mrs. Taylor, cutting Bruh Bruh off.

"Please do not tease the children," she said in a firm tone. I was so glad my teacher stepped in because all eyes were on me. I was so shocked and embarrassed, all I could do is stand there looking awkward. When the embarrassment finally faded."

"I walked up behind Bruh Bruh and said, if you don't leave me alone, I'm going to smack you, but, Bruh Bruh and his friends just laughed and continued to embarrass me everywhere I went."

"He started making stuff up about me. He repeated what I said, but in a high-pitched girly voice. Then at lunch, when I wasn't looking, he took bites off my plate.

Mom, he even brought some of my baby pictures to school and showed them to my classmate even the one that I was naked it on. Mom looked confused at first, then Aydin explained. "The five-month old picture of me laying on my stomach on the changing table," Aydin told mom, I was the worst big brother ever and he was never going back to school again.

Mom said to Aydin; she was sorry that I was thoughtless of his feelings. But, I do love him, and our relationship is too precious to waste.

"Dorian!" mom called out to me, as they enter the living room, "how could you humiliate your little brother in front of his friends?" I took in a deep, scary breath, closed my math book and said, "I was trying to teach him a lesson."

"But son, what you did today in his classroom was inconsiderate of his feelings."

"What!!!" I said to mom with a confused look on my face. "Are you kidding?" Aydin is always inconsiderate of my feelings and my things, but no one lets me express my frustration."

"But, you ruined a very special day for him, and he feels as though you are the worst brother ever," explained mom. "Well, I think he's the worst little brother ever. Sometimes I wished I was an only child again." "Well, you're not, and you need to learn how to get along with your brother," mom said. **"I NEVER HAVE AND I NEVER WILL!!!"** Aydin couldn't believe I said that and he burst into tears.

"How dare you say that about your little brother? Go to your room right now!" ordered mom. I replied, "But, mom, you don't understand." as I gathered up my homework and shoved it inside my backpack.

"Aydin got y'all completely fooled," I shouted. But before I could say anything else, mom interrupted and said, **"Go, to your room now!"** I was so heated, that when I walked passed Aydin, I bumped him really hard, knocking him onto the floor. Mom saw me, and said, "No party for you this weekend."

By this time, I was boiling mad, and the words, you make me sick, rolled off my lips. I didn't know what was going to happen next. And then, mom said, "You're grounded, and that's final." "But that's not fair I've been waiting on this party for three weeks," I growled.

"Did you hear me, go!!!" said mom, "and not another word out of your mouth, do you understand me?" I nodded my head and dragged my feet up the stairs and mumble under my breath to Aydin, "You'll no longer be my brother. Aydin said to me; "I'm sorry Bruh Bruh, I didn't mean to get you in trouble."

"I hate being the baby of the family; it stinks," said Aydin. And he ran up the stair to his room, slammed his door, grabbed his teddy bear and threw himself on the bed sobbing his eyes out.

Mom and Granny were talking in the kitchen. Mom sounded very upset. "I don't know, Mama." She glanced over at granny with tears running down her face and asked, "What's wrong with my children? They rather battle than get along with each other.

It seems like things are getting worse." Granny, then gave mom the biggest mama bear hug she could give and said, "Oh, Tanika," my mom's first name, "all siblings fuel about everything from toys to attention.

"Sibling rivalry is as old as the Bible story about Joseph and his siblings who couldn't get along with each other?

It's a common thing in families. So, don't worry, sweetheart, they would eventually grow out of it and become the best of friends.

Just keep teaching them the best ways to work together and also by building in time to bond over family fun activities that encourage the positive without giving attention to the negative," granny explained to Mom. She also told mom to let us know that she has enough love for the both of us. I was just so glad to hear that.

"You're right Mama, I'm worrying over nothing." After, Mom and granny talked, mom, cooked dinner and made us our favorite yummy mouthwatering dish, chocolate cake. At dinner, mom talked about how much she loved the both of us and can nothing every take that from us. She also said that moms have enough love in their heart and that it never runs out.

CHAPTER 9

At the End of the Day

After dinner and dessert, mom surprised us with a family fun game night on a school night, which was rare. She had created a warm fun space on the living floor and pulled out a few games for us to choose one game to play.

Mom and dad both run the family's business, 7 days a week, but manage to spend time with my little brother and me. So, they turned off their computers and were ready to get beat by their own kids. Mom told us that we could choose one game to play.

So, I let Aydin pick the game to try and make up for what I did to him at school today. I told him I was sorry for embarrassing him in front of his friends. And that I love him and was proud to be his big brother.

Aydin said he was sorry too and, he'll try to do better as a little brother. Then, we hugged each other. because at the end of the day, we are family. And now I understand that mom and dad has enough love for the both of us. And I don't have to worry about being replaced by my little brother.

So, Aydin chose to play the "Pie in Face Showdown Game." He loaded the arms with whipped cream, then Mom and Dad placed their chins on the chin rest and started mashing the button, and it sprung up, and mom got creamed. We laughed at mom, rolling on the floor.

We continued to play until it was bedtime. Dad carried Aydin upstairs on his back, Mom bathed Aydin, he brushed his teeth, then he put on his favorite Black Panther pajama. Mom read him a bedtime story, then tucked him in bed, kissed him on the forehead and said, "We love you with all our heart, son, good night," and they walked toward the door.

"Mom, Dad, WAIT!" shouted Aydin, "how come Bruh Bruh get to stay up?" "Did you learn anything from what we talked about at dinner tonight?" mom asked Aydin."

"Anyway, mom added, "Bruh Bruh is older, and when you get older, you can stay up too. Now, go to bed, you have to go to school in the morning." and she dimed Aydin's bedroom light. "It's not fair, I can't wait until I'm older," he said under his breath as Mom slightly closed the door.

But of course, Aydin wasn't going to take this laying down. He stroked his imaginary beard and said to himself, "No more Mr. Nice Guy, it's time I paid my Bruh Bruh back with a little brotherly prank." Although, mom told me, not to prank Aydin anymore, but, she said nothing about Aydin pranking me.

So, after I pretended to be asleep, Aydin got out of his bed, filled up a cup of water, and he came down to my room, and squeezed through my half-opened door and tiptoed very quietly up to my bed, giggling all the way, hoping he wouldn't bump into anything in the dark and he went to work."

Aydin slowly poured the water onto my bed as close as he could without waking me up, having me to believe in the morning that I had peed in the bed.

So, after he poured the water, he slowly stood on his toes again and moved carefully toward my door. He was almost there when he bumped into my dresser.

He covered his mouth to keep from yelling ooouch!!! And he hopped toward the door, he was trying to be as quiet and careful as he could be, then, he dropped the plastic cup on the floor

Then I sat up in my bed, still half sleep, and shouted the robbers, the robbers, there in the house. Actually, I knew it was my little brother, but by the time I got untangled from my blanket, he was back in his room.

I knew he was peeking through his bedroom door, listening out for me to jump out of my bed and run to the bathroom because my clothes and bed were wet. At first, I wasn't going to play along with it, but then I thought, it's the least I can do for him after I pranked him at school.

And so, I shouted what the heck, loud enough for Aydin to heard me, but low enough for my parents not to hear me. And I took off running down the hallway.

Aydin jumped back in his bed, rolled over on his side and smiled to himself and said, "Yes! Yes! I GOTCHA Bruh Bruh, that'll teach you not to prank me again." By the time I used the bathroom and changed my sleeping gear, Aydin was asleep.

I peeked in his room, smiled and said, "Goodnight little brother. You're the best little brother ever. Even though, we don't always agree, you're still the BEST LITTLE BROTHER EVER."

Printed in the United States
By Bookmasters